Pay No Heed to the Helicopter

Vincent Cavanagh

Guildhall Press

Published in December 2017

Guildhall Press
Ráth Mór Business Centre
Derry
Ireland
BT48 0LZ
info@ghpress.com
www.ghpress.com
T: 077-1502-1188

ISBN: 978 1 911053 30 9

For my wife Nora, my daughter Joan
and granddaughter Asha.

About The Author

Vincent Cavanagh has worked as a GP in Derry since 1964 with experience in Psychiatry in Gransha Hospital and in Queen's University, Kingston, Ontario. He was also Medical Director of the Northlands Centre in Derry since its inception in 1975 until 2010. He was awarded the Macklin Prize for poetry in 2005. Vincent wrote poetry, often late at night, when there was time to ease the problems of the day. And there were many problems over the course of the Troubles. The theme of many of the poems in this collection is related to the distress and suffering of innocent people caught up in dreadful situations not of their own making. Vincent hopes that some of these personal reflections can capture their strength and courage while paying tribute to the memory of some who did not survive.

Acknowledgements

My sincere thanks to: Nora my wife, for her cover painting of Derry at evening as well as for her years of patience and valuable advice with the text, though never after 10.30 at night.

My son Stephen for his skilful and sentient illustrations and the hours of work that these entailed.

Mary Murphy and her invaluable poetry sessions at Thornhill, the first non-medical courses I ever managed to attend.

Raymond Craig for his patience, persistence and sustained encouragement over the last few years. Without him this book would not have happened.

Brother Colm, whose advice years ago was 'look, just do it!'

Paul Hippsley, Peter McCartney, Kevin Hippsley and Joe McAllister at Guildhall Press for the congenial and professionally competent manner in which they have made this book possible.

Contents

ALL THINGS VISIBLE AND INVISIBLE

AROUND THE CORNERS OF THE YEARS

After Eden

Glad to be home from work, he had walked back
To latch the gate. Now he lay motionless,
Strangely crumpled, with unblinking eyes,
Under the bitter pelting of the rain,
No pulse, no breath, no heartbeat, and his life
Washing away with his blood in the roadside runnel.
The neighbour woman who had heard the shots
Wailing again: 'Why don't you do something?
In the name of God, can somebody not do something?'

The rain fell heavily on his upturned face
And in the Winter wind, the wet pine branches
Murmured and swayed against the wild grey sky.
With desperate sirens wailing ever nearer
I closed his eyelids gently, carefully
It seemed the only right thing I could do.

I close them yet, in the dark haunted hours,
Still all that I can do. And then I wake
Soaking with fear and grief and the dismay
That men will lash out blindly. And the shame
Sinks in again, that one of us did this.
But blameless blood is spilt by bent belief
Down all the centuries, in the affairs of men
Outside the garden, since the time of Cain
And will again,
And will again,
And will again.

Beachhead
(In memory of Major Alex Roberts)

As waves come surging in on Pollan Bay
And shatter white upon the rising strand
The eyes of men dim in the dying day

For they remember in the bloody fray
At Normandy, men crawling on the sand
As waves come surging in on Pollan Bay.

From waves of landing craft that led the way
Through waves of bullets from the fortressed land
The eyes of men dim in the dying day,

See not just gun emplacements manned to slay,
But down and round the beach the death-spray fan.
As waves come surging in on Pollan Bay,

Bodies turn in the surf or silent stay
Scattered around and stiffening, hand-to-hand
The eyes of men dim in the dying day.

Voiceless men do not count, and were not they
Lost from the blood-cold hour this war was planned
As waves come surging in on Pollan Bay
The eyes of men dim in the dying day.

Hibakusha

(From the words of Michiko Yamaoka, a survivor of the Hiroshima atomic bombing in 1945)

I was walking, early on the sixth of August
Into the city centre from my house.
The drone of a single plane high up in the sky,
Not in the night-watch hours, but in the morning,
This was the only warning that we got.
It came out of a clear blue sky, the same
As the Twin Towers.
I lost all my face.
The skin hung from my arms like ribbons.
My mother took care of me though she was sick.
I stayed alive for her. She told me to live.
Afterwards, we were told, the mayor said,
'Not even the sound of insects could be heard.'
Years on, my mother died and was cremated.
They found these shards of glass within the ashes,
Embedded, still buried deep inside her body
From the awful force of the explosion.
My body hurts. But now so much more painful
It is to remember what I saw that day,
Although I feel I have to. And to speak of it.
I owe it to my mother. She suffered much.
To tell it is my way of thanking her.

The Entreaty Of Michiko Yamaoka

I know what we did to others.
I have been to China, Hawaii,
Korea, Okinawa and the United States.
I have seen with my own eyes
What we did.
And so now
I can speak
What my mind knows.

I criticize all governments
Including America
And Japan.

I tell all children,
Come to Hiroshima
And see
What war means.

I knew nothing at the time.
But this is how
We were educated.
We were told
Until the day the bomb fell,
That we were winning the war.
Every day we were told,
Die for your country!
That's the terrible power of education.

So I plead with teachers,
Tell children more about the war,
To avoid making the same mistakes again.

I greatly fear
That people will forget.

Out Of Utter Darkness

Out of utter darkness, over the face
Of the broad flowing river, bobbing downstream
There gleamed one hundred and fifty lighted candles,
Each in their white hand-folded paper boat.
We stood on the damp quay, watching them grow nearer,
Caught in uneasy sadness around that day
Now thirty year before, when the world shook
And the very air splintered and exploded.

'What the hell… what in God's name is that?'
The shouting wild, a hoarse and frantic voice
Behind us, questioning; a pointing arm,
Finger like a pistol. Clutched in his other hand
An open bottle of South African wine
Camouflaged in a crushed brown paper bag.
Speechlessly and rigid, he stared and gestured
At the scattered lights moving on the waters,
A field of stars in the innocence of night.

Staggering sideways from the derelict shed
The winos used, his battered soulmate circled
A safe distance around our contact point,
Sweating with sickness, hollow-eyed and scared.

'It marks the anniversary of the bomb
That fell on… that destroyed… Hiroshima;
You know, the atom bomb. So many died.
The lights out on the water are for them.

We light them in their memory tonight.
One candle burns for every thousand killed.'
'Then you can see the lights… you see them, too!'
He stumbled back towards his shaking friend
And put his arm around the suffering man.
'It's alright, it's alright, s'alright,' he said.
'He can see it, too. They see it, too.
I tell you, they can see… here, here, take this.'
And passed the careful bottle, tenderly
And gripped it in his hand to help him drink
Like a soaked sponge, held on the point of a spear.

Stripped of all pride, unsteady on their feet,
In the unstable shelter of each other,
They went again on their abandoned way
As dim flames fading on the whispering river.

Afterwards

As we emerge into the light
And our sight begins to clear
We stumble our sorry, white-faced way
Out of the rubble of forty years.

Dried blood on our faces and on our hands,
Red stains of our land's disgrace,
Lost limbs, lost lives, lost balanced minds
With what name do they brand this place?

For some of us did inhuman things
In seething rage and senseless.
And decent, fragile, fearful men
Lay low and silent in their trenches.

They butchered us, we butchered them,
And nothing can now be hidden.
By what name shall we call this place?
And what, under God, will we tell the children?

Hector And Andromache

Hector had hard-learned to bear his sword
Bravely in the foremost line of battle
And thereby won great honour for his father
And himself. Marching with men of Troy,
And in the desperate defence of Troy,
This resolution greatest in his heart,
To save his dearest wife from slavery,
From degradation.

But she pleaded thus,
'Your bravery will be the death of you.
My people all are slain. You are my father,
Brother and loving husband. Do not go
And make your wife a widow, your son an orphan.'

He lifted high and kissed the child and prayed.
'May you bring joy into your mother's heart.
O Zeus, grant that my son be strong and when
He grows to manhood, wise and sure of eye
And strong in arm. Then let the people say:
This noble youth is greater than his father.'

He left the hall and she wept bitterly
And all the women wept and mourned for Hector
In his own house while he was yet alive,
Certain, that he could not escape his enemies,
Nor from the battle, ever again return.

Kathleen
(Creggan pantomime, 1980)

My heart was high at the pantomime
In St Mary's Hall tonight
The children sang and the children danced
Through music and colour and light.

Out of the wind and the icy rain
Away from the sodden streets
Out of the world of the fearful dark,
Safe in the sudden heat.

The stage was bright in the darkened hall
We clapped and cheered together
Our hearts were surrounded and lifted up
And held, it seemed, forever.

With wide-eyed wonder the children watched
As the hero walked hand-in-hand
With the beautiful princess, his only love,
To Never-Never land.

And I wept and shuddered and wept again
For the pain in the land of roses
He was moved to the Crumlin Road today
And the coalhouse is full of explosives.

The Flowers Are Dying

He gripped the back wall, six inches wide
In a street full of gas, in besieged Bogside
And his fingers were mashed by a rubber bullet:
At twenty-four.

In Rosemount he looked out the window to see
What was going on and blindingly
He lost his eyes to a rubber bullet:
At twelve years old.

He searched for his son in the riot's heat
To keep him away out of William Street
And he lost half his skull to a rubber bullet:
At fifty-four.

Even in anger, confusion or fear
You shouldn't expect to get anywhere near
To losing your life to a rubber bullet:
At fifty-four.

We saw them all in this awful state
And our protests pressured a change by the state
So they started again with a plastic bullet:
Like years before.

The Ballad Of The Garage Man

There was a decent family man
Worked hard to earn a pound
He bought a modest garage
On the outskirts of the town

One night the balaclavas came
They threatened him with guns
And demanded the week's takings
That the bank was waiting on.

Now the experts in security
All tell you to comply
With threats from men with weapons
That it's madness to defy

So he handed them the money
And they fled into the night
While he stood there shamed and angry
And still shaking with the fright.

'Don't worry,' said the family.
'You're home safe, with your health.
After all, it's only money.'
But he studied to himself

Thinking, what kind of a father
Leaves his pride in smithereens
For a bunch of so-called gunmen
That are likely in their teens?

And what kind of example
Am I giving to my kids
So that when they get in trouble
They'll surrender, like I did?

Soon after that they came again
Their weapons he defied
So they took the money after
They had shot him in the thighs

And they pumped the petrol all around
As he lay in the mud
And burned the business to the ground
And burned his trail of blood.

'You should have given them the cash
And played it by the rules.'
They called their father foolish
And as stubborn as a mule.

So the sons grew up and left him
And the daughters changed their name.
The wife stayed on, though woebegone
And it never was the same.

The Message
(The Bogside, 1975)

Here, wee son,
Run away round the corner
To the shop, Pet,
And get your granny
Ten cigarettes.
Here's the money.
Tell him it's Players,
He'll know
It's me.
Don't go out on the road
Or up the square.
Mind that oul' swine
In number nine
And Holy Marie
In thirty-three
And watch for you know who,
The Shootin' Star
In case he leaves the bar
With too much taken.
Don't be long now.
I'll be waitin'
D'ye hear me?
Away you go
And if you need
I'll get you a piece
For your supper.
Run on now
Like a good boy
And pay no heed
To the helicopter.

William

(In memory of Surgeon Lieutenant William A Cavanagh who went down with the battlecruiser HMS *Repulse* on 10 December 1941 in the South China Sea)

When I was only ten years old, I found
A bunch of letters, still in dusty envelopes,
Held by a faded ribbon, in a box
In Drumaweir House, up in the attic room.
Letters from good people to my grandmother,
On hearing the reported death of William,
The telegram regretting 'killed in action'
Her son, my uncle, in the South China Sea.

William, who knew the sight and smell of boats
Piers, fish, ropes, nets and tar, and bladderwrack,
And lived among them since his boyhood days,
Played on the yellow strand, swam in the sea,
Dived through the waves and saw the waving banks
Of seaweed slowly moving with the tide
Over the rippled surface of the sand
And underwater sunlight, dim and green.
And sometimes in the full tide evening's calm
The wonder-sight of slate-grey, shining fish.

He who loved parties, dancing, playing songs
On the piano, or the dulcitone
And flirted musically, had smiles returned
By breathless, bright young ladies of Moville,
With bobbed hair, A-line frocks and thoughtful eyes,
Playing new records on the gramophone
And then, the latest thing in Drumaweir,
Hearing the news on brand-new wireless sets,
Ominous amongst the danceband tunes.

How terrible a strangeness to end up
Steaming to the north of Singapore,
Here, in the perilous South China Sea
In huge explosions, wild gunfire, torpedoes,
Smoke and shouting, flames and diving planes,
Tending to burnt and bleeding, dying men,
On the hot surface of the tilting deck
With work and fear and horror all in one.
Then one again, the underwater sun,
The great grey broken warship sinking down
Beneath the burning surface of the sea,
Fractured, tormented, groaning, powerless,
Settling heavily onto the sea bed,
With banks of seaweed waving in the tide
And yellow sand and silence.

Years later I met a lady, and she said,
'You must be William's nephew,' and she paused,
Moved closer, closer to me and her eyes
Moistened, and misted over, and her trembling.
'I see his face, oh God, you're very like my William.'
And she slowly veiled her face
Beneath her hands and softly moved away
Into the garden, through the apple trees
Her white hair gleaming where the Summer light
Dappled the glowing grass through shining leaves
And branches swaying in the living air,
Lost in her thoughts and seeing none of this.

To measure up to honour such as yours,
The risking and the losing of your life,
There are no words.
Can there be consolation, just to know
Your name is written up in monuments
In Happy Valley Cemetery in Hong Kong;

On the memorial on Plymouth Hoe;
At Greencastle's new Maritime Museum
With embossed names of all the other men
Of Inishowen, taken by the sea;
On the bright granite at the family grave
Of your own people, up at Ballybrack
And on the big shop window at Drumaweir
Engraved there by yourself, when very young,
Using, it's said, your mother's diamond ring
To prove for certain, you could write on glass?

You were last seen out on the open deck
Tending to scalded, wounded, desperate men.
And did you feel the General Absolution
That brought some crumb of comfort to the family?
And do you know that Europe and the East
Remain at peace, for these last sixty years
And that your campaign medals still stay more
Than precious to this further generation?
That is, when we remember to remember,
That life is built on those who've gone before,
And liberty is earned. And at great cost.

In the South China Sea, the great ships lie,
The *Prince of Wales*, alongside the *Repulse*.
You are still resting there, in the half-light,
Where this great host of young men's lives were lost
And yours lost, too, in the December cold
Of 1941, so far from home
Aged only thirty-three, and not grown old.

In the world's countless souls who met their death
In war, there is no heartbeat now, no breath,
But maybe something of you, feels and sees
And wanders, wistful, through the apple trees.

Autumn River

The path, grey evening river, easing quiet
October, with my swallows gone and geese
Returning in straight and sounding arrow lines.
These many weeks I have walked, twilight and dark,
With few about to feel the fading year,
Through pools and mud or frosted frozen grass,
To strengthen and recover; clean and cool
The heated breath and tender wounds of illness,
Regain the suppleness of limb and thought;
A journey which in truth is made of time
Not reason, knowing that the odds have changed
Again and shortened, like these Autumn days.

The flocks of birds observe me on the edge
Of their perspective, of their personal space
And gently, without seeming, move along.
I watch them, common gulls, blackheaded gulls,
Small waders, oystercatchers flying fast
In black and brilliant white with piping cries,
All single notes, as from a piccolo,
And then in herds grazing on shortened grass
Or through the mudflat's black and light reflections.
And who would think to cross the reeds and find
Rock doves on mud and hooded crows. And who
Has ever grasped the beauty of a rook

But now I see they loft into the wind
And speed-glide smooth and low above the water
Skating the wind. Crows elegantly know
Their way about. I see the cormorants dive

Or stand on weedy rocks as crucified.
I watch the redshanks, wading on the tide edge
And then their sudden swirl and flashing flight.
I am absorbed in light and air and water,
Held in the vigour of this fresh-found world.

The evening train from Belfast rattling by
On rails which skirt the river's eastern bank;
The rising plane now banking left for London
Cause no alarm in this winged population.
My neighbour, the grey heron, old and wise,
Beneath the towering span of the Foyle Bridge,
At his well-favoured fishing place, he stands
In the still tide pool, mirrored, motionless,
Observing all. If I keep walking on,
All's well. But should I stop, return his gaze,
He waits, debates a minute and then stretches
His great grey wings and lifts a little way,
Fades like the misty memory of a fever,
Further away, away, away.

Second Sight

A stiffened old Yank
With a drink and a dollar
Aggrieved to the pin
Of his Inishowen collar

Come home to retrace
Stubborn steps of his youth
And to face the old place
With its truths and half-truths.

Then the crumbling stone walls
That thatch long fallen through
And young trees colonizing
The hearth and the flue

Thick bushes and grass
Growing over the ground
Where the garden was worked,
Now a shape with no sounds.

The plucking of silence
A harp with no strings
Just jackdaws and rooks
And a beating of wings
With an instant to grasp
The erosion of things.

Caroline Lucy
(In memory of my grandmother who died in
Drumaweir House in 1942)

I see a garden red and blue
And yellow where the roses grew
Such blossoms with green glowing stems
Where, kneeling, she had planted them.

I see the garden deep with snow
Another morning long ago
A jet-black hearse with horses two,
Grey church and graveyard lined with yew.

The big slim wheels made slushy tracks
From Drumaweir to Ballybrack
While all the people walked behind
To bid farewell to Caroline

With solemn bell and quiet blend
Of sadness, at her journey's end
But surging June brought hollyhocks
And poppies and forget-me-nots.

On The Electrodynamics Of Moving Bodies
(For Q, my friend, who has knowledge beyond the rest of us)

We chanced to meet on Princes Street
Outside the Georgian door of his
Old home. A whirl of gusting leaves
On the dry paving stones of Autumn.
'Look at all these leaves,' he said,
'My father always swept them up.
I'd see him with the yard brush here
When I came wandering home from school.
Father, there's no real need to sweep
Them up, they're always whisked away.
The wind takes them.
"It occupies me,
Keeps me busy. And they dance
For me, round me, tell me what way
The wind is blowing."
And you know,
After he had been taken from us
I went and did the same myself.
Swept up the leaves, like my father did.
I always loved the sound of shoes
Rustling through the leaves and wind
Whispering together like a symphony;
Siosarnach, in the ancient tongue.'

Think what you've touched, the whispering sounds,
The leaves, your father, the Autumn wind,
The dying year, continuum,
The rustle, music, *siosarnach.*
Don't lose it, old friend.

Write it down.
'Ah no,' he said, 'ah no, because
I'm a psychotic, as you know,
And you will see that I avoid
Contact with people, conversation,
In case I frighten them with thoughts
They can't accept and won't allow
The traceries the wind conceives
The glistening galaxies of leaves.'

But psychotic is just a general word
Has books and books of interpretations.
If Einstein hadn't been a bit
Psychotic, he would never have thought
That time might slow with acceleration.
That seemed insane, to the sane of us
But in the end, the man was right.
And so it may take a different view
A crazy angle from afar
To see things as they really are.

You never know what wonderful
Insights and meanings you may have
Maybe as crazy as Albert had
Or even crazier, like Niels Bohr.
'Prediction is difficult,' Niels has said,
'Particularly of the future.'
But think about it, concentrate,
So that the thought may not escape,
So that ideas will constellate.

The fall flows down and round the street
With Georgian doors, now painted red

And black and yellow, like the leaves
Swirling around the sweeper's shoes

And as he faster, faster, sweeps
And looks for points of reference
The houses stretch, grow tall and thin.
Moments are lost, the leaves float up
And all the clocks in Princes Street
Slow to a song of childhood time,
A boy meandering home from school
Lilting a lapsing rhyme, self-taught
With something wonderful in his eyes
And something radiant in his thoughts.

Prediction is difficult, we agree,
Particularly of the past
But if he writes it as he sees
And knows things as they really are
Then we move closer to the vast
And dreamy seasons of the stars.

Hippocrates Of Kos

(For Dr Peter Fallon, retired 12 July 1996 after
48 years a physician)

Listen and hear the best of doctors teach
The leading edge of knowledge. Watch them chart
The changing context, always slow advancing.
This can be learned and is the easier part.

No-one can step in the same morning twice,
The art-song that you sing reflects each cue
Of relevance and meaning, for no text
Ever contained a patient that you knew.

It is not possible to tell in words
The thousand ties of understanding, each
Unique and tempered by the fragile touch
Of conscious contact, aching within reach.

This art can be achieved; cannot be taught.
This changeless warmth is mankind's and has eased
All down the ages, since the first physician
With steadied fingers, felt the first disease.

For life is short and yes, the art is long,
Occasions fleeting, judgements difficult,
Experience deceptive. This being seen
Then let men honour him, his life, his work.

Beyond Doubt

(For Tom Mullarkey)

My mind on him, whom I have known so long,
Circled by dark matters all around,
No surgery, no further fighting drugs
But opiates and finely focused rays.
I walk the river path with searching steps
Prospecting in the deep and restless night.
Under the soaring columns of Foyle Bridge,
Turning, I see how, banked up on the hills
This fierce old city lies, ablaze with lights,
A cluster of stars, defiant in the darkness,
Vibrant with possibility, not hesitant
Upon the step of the tremendous question.

Leaves Turning

Along dry paths she dawdles
Her two small dogs, as always
Slowly, in the park;
Today through thistledown,
With wisps of scented wood smoke
Spicing the Autumn air.

The clinics now are ended
No visits for a year;
No further insubstantial rays
A whole long drawn-out year,
No solace for the twelve-month
Unclenching here.

Evening grows grey and quiet
And under a settled sky
The rushes fade; dry grasses
And dwindling yellow vetchling
Edging the year's advance.
From the stretch of river meadow
Fast food and their last dance
The swallows are suddenly gone.

She scans the clouded heavens
For skeins of whooper swans,
Listens for their coming,
For beating wings from the north,
To tick the leaves turning,
To sign the days shortening,
To mark the changing season,

The huge moon over Altnagelvin,
The harvest,
The gathering in.

Scope

Beneath screened strip lights
In the high-tech curtained space,
I surface at an angle of forty-five degrees
In my backless green gown,
Floating, half-dreaming
After the scope.
The nurses, sure and practised
With kind hands, deft words,
Glance swift half-smiles.
They read the electronic vital signs
And organise hot tea and toast,
Two slices, buttered and triangulated,
Tasting of home, almost.
'Rest on a while,' they say.
'We've called your wife just now
And in an hour's time
She'll come and get you.'
'That's good.
Thank you.'

The surgeon strides along the ward
Purposeful, white-coated,
Charts gripped beneath his arm
And Sister by his side,
They seem controlled and serious
A look I know,
Signalling the case discussed,
Decisions made, the words agreed.
They walk along the beds.
They stop with me.

And then at once
He tells me all he's found
And where he thinks that we should go from here.
She soothes us both in this abrupt
Reality and unreality.
Thank you.

I rest on as advised with lowered lids
And try, time and again
To search the hazy road ahead.
Tomorrow and tomorrow.
And then he comes once more.
'I see your wife is here for you.'
Then soft-voiced, hesitating,
'Would it be helpful…
If I talked with her?'

Sober Reflections

Harry, the drinker,
Saddened now and scarred
By years of foolishness,
Flayed by the truth of Family Day,
Sat taciturn over coffee and cigarettes
When all the relatives had gone away.
In sudden need, he said,
'It's hard to see yourself, I mean,
What you really are, spiritually,
Never mind mentally.
I have heard clergymen often, years ago
Preaching in solemn services, on religious things,
Sin and Commandments, Death and Resurrection
And "we must all repent" – that sort of thing.
Now they talk of New Theology
And Spirituality. Well,
I never was a religious man, myself
And haven't crossed a granite porch
For maybe twenty years.
But still,
The first step towards sobriety
Can't be put off again.
And so, so be it.
I'm working at understanding what they tell me,
Although, as my father used to say,
It's like driving nails in a fog.
For even during serious discussions here,
My mind, in spite of me,
Slips off to peaceful places
Where I have known strange quiet

Like Strangford or the Erne
But most of all, Lough Neagh.

'Lord, I remember waiting,
Listening through the end of night,
For the beating of wings,
The ducks returning.

'And floating there
Alone,
On flat black silent waters
Watching the massive sky,
Slowly sensing clearly and more clearly
Eternal darkness,
Streaked by stray meteorites,
Emblazoned by innumerable stars,
Trembling and sparkling in the immensity.
And then the emptiness,
The want.

'I lay so many times, paralysed with wonder,
Awed by the momentary blaze of recognition
Of a different order,
Of impossible complexity.

'Startled, as always, by sudden wings
I grip and aim the gun,
Firing at fleeting shadows,
Reload, fire again
Shouts, hammer blows, blood,
Splashes of reality.

'I drive the Belfast road
And as the morning grows
There lingers only a sense of loss,

Echoes of understanding,
A striving to recall again
Something beyond remembering,
Out of my grasp again,
Elusive, tantalizing, fundamental.

'As I've said before, I'm not
A religious man myself
But do you think it's possible
That this is what they're going on about,
The clergymen.
Could this be what they mean?'

Genesis
(For Mr Brennan, the dedicated teacher who gave me rare and much-needed encouragement)

It was once in Rialto Hospital
The poet lay on the brink
Of easeful death with his laboured breath,
In the haze of his fondness for drink.

His friends gathered round and advised him:
'Grangegorman's the place for you,
Away up and talk to the doctors there
For they know a trick or two.'

And the poet churned thoughts in his thinking
And sourly, he turned in the bed.
'What can a psychiatrist do for a poet?'
In a gravelly voice, he said,

'Go an' get me a naggin of Paddy
With a shot glass to take it neat.'
But they solemnly sat like a bunch of flowers
So the poet stalked back to sleep.

And he dreamed of the whins of Mucker,
The winds and the weeping skies;
Of the road that runs from Inniskeen
And from them that would criticize.

And the dream-road led on to Baggot Street
And to Grafton Street, where he sowed
And harrowed the urban smallholders
From Rathmines to Raglan Road.

On Raglan Road where he met again
His girl with the long dark hair
And he wakened pleased with his breathing eased
And a poem with her own name there.

O, he struggled back into the sun again
Transcending all things banal,
Since he learned not to care, in the silence there
On his seat on the Grand Canal.

Hill Farmer

In fierce anger sometimes;
Often in near despair
I make a brief rough prayer.
Send me a new idea
A thought, an inspiration
To maybe transform everything.
There has to be a flash
Something which will make
All the longed-for difference
An escape from this descent
A path out of the lowlands,
Seeking for oblivion
In an empty bottle
In a half-empty glass.
Time and again I sleepwalked
Wakened to disaster,
No memory of what I'd done
But knowing it was bad
Seeing the same sickness
But now, no more of that.
Today, no more of that.

In abstinence, nights are hard
And sleep is not a friend.
I wake in sweaty darkness
And cannot rest. On feverish
Impulse, I leave the house
And climb the grassy slopes
For every hillside track
Is known to me in light

Or no light and I climb
Until I reach 'The Boulder',
My ancestor erratic,
My seat of sanctuary.
There I can hear the sheep
Move round me in the night.
They all know me, my sheep
They come to try the grass,
Graze around my feet
And I welcome them in
With soft undertones;
'Here now, here now, sheep.'
And it is daybreak lovely,
Something apart,
This touch of trust is lovely
To an unwedded heart.

The night is moonlight quiet
But the odd car growling
Away down the far road
Beyond the silent lake
And the afterlife of day
Brings a strange calm within
The browsing of my flock
In that grey light, before
The urgency of sunrise;
A peace in my head
Even though I cannot see
A single day ahead;
Not even a day ahead.

The Doctor: 1943

(In memory of my father who told me this)

Red dog roses by the whitewashed wall
White turf smoke streaming smoothly
From the neighbour's chimney.
The sun rising.
He stood on the doorstep, bag in hand,
Seeing with night-weary eyes
The quiet fields, the lanes,
Whitethorn hedges,
The brilliance of morning
On the estuary of the Foyle.
The tractor spluttering to life
At the gable end
Startled him,
His mind on matters
Deeper than yesterday or tomorrow.
For it is a terrible, terrible thing
To leave a home on the third day
And behind you
A stillborn infant
And a dead mother.

Red roses, morning sun,
The taste of ashes.
This cannot be right,
Nor the acceptance of it.

The Girls Of Aberfoyle

For nearly forty years I saw
The sun shine down on Aberfoyle
On brown and black and yellow hair
Of all the girls at Aberfoyle

Who kept it going, made it work,
Who helped us, kept us in our place,
Who listened, reassured and solved
And sometimes smiled and gave us space.

Who slipped a patient in the door,
Not always strictly necessary,
But often serious, showing their
Intuitive, instinctive caring.

Who took abuse from some of these
Our wounded ones, with mental pain,
Our saddened, angry, fragile ones,
Then wept a while and overcame.

And as the surgeried years eased past,
Who lived, grew older and became
Parents, just like us older ones
And learned to take and shoulder blame

And slowly, steadily became
Connective tissue of all parts
That held the eyes and ears and hands,
That held the breathing and the heart.

And times will change and faces change
The years engulf us
And are gone
And in our ever-changing world
One certain thing, this work goes on

And when another forty years
Have passed, there will be other coils
Of brown and black and yellow hair
To shine in the sun,
At Aberfoyle.

In homage to our fifteen working secretaries, their predecessors over the years, and especially to the doctors' wives who took the out-of-hours practice phone calls since 1945. Written at the time of my retirement from General Practice.

Two Roads Diverge

Abruptly, the flight to Manchester was called
Passports and boarding cards from wallets drawn
We made quick fumbled gestures of farewell
'And don't forget …' I said,
And they were gone.

Back on the motorway, passing to the north
I glance across the water and I see
Over the grey, unlovely Belfast Lough
Their plane ascending, parallel to me.

We sped together near a mile and then
The motorway curved uphill and to the west
Their plane banked to the east, our paths diverged
On to untrodden ways and acid tests.

Perhaps in the rubble fields of Liverpool
Or Manchester's grit and inequality
Then maybe they will think of home and feel
The fierce warmth of this small unflinching city

And also see green mountains, country roads,
The sanctity of Mamore, with way below
Leenan, Dunaff, Tullagh and Malin Head
With Tory, west over the tidal flow

So I will go, sit over Leenan Bay
And think slow thoughts of severance and loss,
Learning the while, how way leads on to way
As parting brings a kindness and a cross.

Timetable

The table where I dine
Is made of wood
Crafted with sure hands
By the maker.

I scan the shining surface with my eyes.
My fingers touch attractors in the grain.
Constellations in the living timber.

Intrinsic to the grain,
Complex, exquisite,
Are molecules of oak
And therein atoms
Shimmering, holding, dancing,
As ancient,
As immense,
As distant as Andromeda.

My vision but distracted by perspective,
I could see things enlarge
Until they become tiny.

All this in time
Is common as sawdust
To the carpenter's son.

As We Forgive Them

A dark and bitter day.
In Bishop Street the stinging rain
Lashing the Courthouse,
The tall columns, the steps of stone.
Groups of tired people
Cramming the cold hall and narrow corridors
With huddled consultations in bare side rooms.
Damp clothes and anxious words,
Pale sunless legal skin in gowns and wigs and suits.
Murmured opinions and advices,
Covert muttering, strained faces
Waiting.

The broken man I knew,
Confined unseen, held in the cells below,
Charged by the police, the social workers,
Of crimes against his children;
Unspeakable;
Bleak.

Through the security, the heavy outside doors
There came a face,
Gone away these many years.
A grown man now but drained, dishevelled
From a painful journey.
Uneasy recognition in his eyes
He fumbled through the groups and spoke to me.
'He has done terrible things,' he said,
'He has broken the laws of God and Man
He has fractured our family

He has shamed our name.
I did not want to come…
But I have come
Because he is my father
And I must
At least
Be here with him.'

Apotheosis

Cosmologists hypothesise
The universal presence
Of Dark Matter.
That massive shadow
Somehow invisible,
Asserting power,
Mystery,
Vibrancy
And from which is hung
All ordinary matter
And thence
All life.
It radiates no light,
No signs,
No wonders,
But we can sense that it is there,
The pull of it
Is everywhere.
Without this presence
There is no existence
For without it was made
Nothing that was made.

Where it wills
The wind blows
And you hear the sound
But you do not know
Whence it comes
Or whither it goes.

Crex Crex

We came to Tory's towering rocks
In life's unfailing evening fall
Eager to recognise again
The covert corncrake's aching call.

Sounding away that Summer night,
The steady throb, the double rasp
Came resonating down the years
From hideouts in the sheltering grass.

The ferryman, with wind-swayed eyes
Opened his *uisce beatha* store
And to the tossing wine-dark sea
He poured a mouthful overboard.

'This drop is for the wee folk. When
The bottle's opened on the ship
You make the offering, just in case
You might not get to finish it.

'And for the ageless islander
Who plays a nameless melody
To lull the blazing sunset down
Into this circling western sea.'

The rise and setting of the sun
The corncrake in the middle ground,
The whiskey in the living waves,
The wee folk, beyond sight or sound,

Such things are measureless. We touch
On unimaginable streams,
Struggle, survival and regrowth
Beyond the gravity of dreams.

Once Upon A Time

Look around in wonder. All of this
Is shaped from stardust. And all living things
By natural selection have survived
Since the first cells developed and the fittest
Crawled from the oceans into a violent world.
Out from the fusion furnace in screaming stars
Came the essential acids that were needed
To congregate in beauty, self-assemble
Into the elegance of the double helix.
White radiation from a billion suns
Streamed out until it warmed and clothed in light
Those planets with the luck of Goldilocks
With everything just right. And there was life;
A mystery of science, but not the same
As mysteries of religion, those superstitions
That tether mankind in ignorance and forbid
Him search across the cosmos for his destiny.
We don't require a God-head to explain
The existence of the universe, or life
And just as well, because there is no God.

God in his brown robe, sat deep in thought
With chin in hand upon the mountain side,
For an unending time and then he sighed
An infinite sigh, a sigh unto eternity.
He lifted Man and sat him on his knee.
He put his arm around him, cleared his throat
And said, 'Alright, we'll go through it again.
Once upon a time, before all time,
In the beginning, I created heaven and earth

And darkness was upon the face of the deep
And my spirit moved over the face of the waters.
I said, let there be light, and there was light.
Evening came and morning; the first day.
And evening came and morning; the seventh day.
After I warned you of the forbidden fruit,
The dangerous apples of the tree of knowledge,
I rested long; perhaps I overslept.
And so again I ask you; watch with me
And I will show the pathways through the stars
And all things visible and invisible.'

Little Faith

(For Jeanie McDaid)

A small bent body, moving slowly, awkwardly
Old raincoat to her ankles, brown and worn,
Grey wisps of hair escaping from her headscarf,
Bearing three plastic bags in her white hands
Up the long hill. Her tired hips protest.
Childbearing was easier. She pauses, stops.
Her face is pale with effort. On her white brow
A thumb has marked a shocking scar of black
For this is now Ash Wednesday and today
She is instructed, as down all the years,
That she, a penitent, is made of dust
And unto dust she shall return again.
Unquestioning, she wears the badge of shame
Although, in faith she falters, full of grace.

For I have seen her, when the April moon
Had traced a glittering path across the Foyle,
Walking on silver water, with another,
Taller and somehow mistier, stooping over
Gently to speak, and carrying her groceries,
Startling the seagulls, on the short way home.

Photograph Of Norrie

February outlines the black trees with damp grey light.
Norrie, frail and stooped now, sits by the fire,
Warm in her armchair,
Grown too large for her.
The centre of the family,
The history of this place is written round her;
Ten children, two world wars, eight popes,
Partition, civil war, the Troubles,
Widowhood.
She knows injustice, prejudice
The bending of ideals
The unfolding of life
The prayer
The consolations.
And one day showed me
A picture in a book of local history.
This placed her
A wedding guest of fifty years ago
On the steps of a mansion
One of the many built along the Foyle
By the great families of the city.
And I remember a red spark,
Just the once
When, with teeth-clenched anger,
'Yes,' she said,
'And all built on the backs of the workers.'
Silence
And then,
'Goodnight and God bless you.'

Pilgrimage
(The story of San Girolamo)

'There is no need for priests,'
He said,
'Nor bishops either.'
A long pause in the warm and terraced night
Gazing down over Florence.

'I'm a very old man,' he said,
And soft-voiced,
Talked of his long priesthood,
The chaplaincy in Europe, World War II
Again in the Korean War
Then on and on to minister in Texas
Where dollars in their plenty were made offerings
But prayers were not.

'I'm eighty-six,' he said,
And he looked it then,
Moist-eyed, downcast,
Saying quietly with clenched fists,
'You see – the people feel the urge
For contact with their Creator,
But no-one can do it for them.
No-one!
They have to do it by themselves.
By themselves!'

The hum of city traffic from miles below
Filled the silence
Like a long intake of breath.

‘Over the years, I’ve learned,’
I said at last,
‘That old men, coming near life’s end,
And looking back on actions done and not done,
See only darkened days
And things they are ashamed of
As everyone will do.
No longer do they see the efforts made,
The hard work done,
The grace that came,
The ripples of good still spreading,
Widening out beyond their ken.
I sense in you
The sadness of old age.
It is a personal, preordained Gethsemane
Long defined, inevitable nearly;
It may be sent to try us.

‘So let us stay awake,
Here above this ancient olive grove
And watch an hour,
Together.’

Next day was brighter.
His pilgrimage renewed
He talked non-stop and smiled a lot
On the bus to Siena
Where we drank a little wine
On sunny steps
In the Piazza del Campo.
The night before had passed.

All this was years ago.
Now as I age myself
And finding difficulties in the Nicene Creed,
Dogmas that became undone;
Disquiet looking back,
Doubts which have no answer now
That mutter in the waking night,
Closed is that route of counsel.
I cannot leave the garden on my own.
And so,
My old friend
If you can hear me now
Let us sit again
And once more watch one hour
While the world is hushed and holy.
Talk with me.
Give me your priestly nudge towards first light.
The details are unimportant.

Samson And Delilah

Oh Samson was the strongest man
His strength lay in his hair.
Delilah shaved it off in waves
And left him weak and bare.

Then the Philistines gouged out his eyes,
Enslaved him, kept him low
But they forgot to keep it cut
And the hair began to grow.

And at the great temple gathering
They chained him to the pillars
But he shook them round till the roof came down
On Samson the great mass-killer.

For he slew three thousand Philistines
And included in that number
He killed himself, with the fervent stealth
Of the world's first suicide bomber.

The Eleventh Station

(For Sister Aloysius)

One morning in our convent school
I watched the children draw
The nailing to the cross.
One small girl drew the scene and paused and then
Added an angry crowd,
Foregathered, ready,
Hefting their heavy hammers in their hands.

I was surprised, was troubled, then dismayed
But from then on
My understanding changed
And that is why in Steelstown Church
You see that, breaking with convention,
I have painted shadowy background figures
Dark with menace.
They are us, mankind
And I am there.
One of the many, able to do great good,
Capable, too, of violence and hate,
Just as she showed me, fifty years ago.
Then as now.

Yes,
I remember Joan.

In memory of my sister Joan who died at home on 20 January 1947 aged seven years.

The Merchant Kings

(Or IOR: *Instituto per le Opere di Religione* – the Vatican Bank)

In poverty, a child is born
Three kings rode through the eastern morn
With precious gifts, that caused a stir,
Of gold and frankincense and myrrh.

While shepherds watched and angels sang
And praise throughout the heavens rang,
The gifts were snatched, for rules were lax
At IOR and Goldman Sachs.

Three kings of finance and aromatics
Defying all apologetics
Cornered the lot, and thus had shown us
How they retrieve their annual bonus.

For rising tides don't lift all boats
It's inequality that floats
And this is the lesson that is told
Of myrrh and frankincense and gold.

Transitions

The illness came and went;
Hard fought and held at bay
For fourteen lonely years,
But urged to persevere
With finely focussed rays
And bitter treatments,
He survived it all
Though each time through the bedroom window
In grim withdrawal
The Reaper glowered darkly,
'I'll be back.'

Now as the end of days approached again,
Scythed and laid low
He murmured, 'I suppose
That it's as good a day as any for it.'
And having been so close to death
So many times
You can't ignore it.
That twilight presence becomes familiar,
Like a friend, almost.

I have no fear of dying now
For recent times I reckon
It's the fear that torments
Like a crown of thorns
And so,
With slow acceptance in these last few days
I gently ease it off.
The sharp pain fades
And I can smile on death.

And although, as before,
The unknown beckons,
There, safely stored away
In the back marches of my mind
I can unearth the full range of a life
Back to the beginning
And grasp the hazy memory
Of the way it was
Before that first fresh morn,
When most of us were afraid
To be born.

Watercolour

A half-used lane, truly more like a path
Along the field's edge, worn in the wet ground
With flooded puddles, filled up to the black
Serrated ledges of the tractor tracks.
The cows' deep hoof prints, homing for the byre
Through tufted grass, like post-holes from the past,
Bog-cotton lighting up besoms of rushes
Beneath old fence posts hung with rusted wires
And all the laneway veering north and down
Between the hill brow and high fuchsia bushes.
I gazed a while and then departed thence
But kept the muddy vision with me since
And painted it in watercolour tints
Green solitude, white light and brown content,
Leaves and coarse grass, bog-cotton, as they leant
Through shining mud and pools of innocence.

St Augustine

St Augustine
Grown tired of lustin'
Put away his wife
That he had no trust in

Wrote his confession
About sex and sinnin'
And besmirched the lives
Of five billion women

And after he'd done
His misogynist worst
They made him a Father
Of the Church.

The Birdman Of Meadowbank
(For George)

Derry docks in deep December
With stinging rain over the windswept walk
Along the grey-tossed river;
The air unclear, sleet-misted,
The east bank barely visible.
There, in the turbulence of the storm,
A tall patrician figure moved
In his long grey raincoat,
The unlatched belt knotted behind,
White hair blowing like the waves below.
With all the solemn presence of an Isaiah
He stood with dignity
Alone but for his black-haired dog.
From three bulging plastic bags
He broke off lumps of bread,
Tossing them through the chill air,
Some onto the dock,
Some onto the cold grey waters.

On the ground around his feet
Were sixty pigeons
Surging tightly back and forth
And muttering to themselves.
Above his head, scores of clamouring gulls;
Blackheaded gulls they were, in their Winter white
Circling, darting, diving, screaming hunger.
His quiet smooth-haired dog
Stayed demure and innocent at his feet,
Gazing away with black incurious eyes

Everywhere except at the outrageous birds
Contending all around him and above.
'They need to be fed,' he said,
'They get desperate when there's nothing to eat.
They always see me when I'm walking here
And swarm in from the tide
Like Pennyburn Church on Sundays.'

He fed the multitude
With five small loaves
And yet, the bags were bulging still
When he and the dog walked off
Steadily down the river walk
Beside the white-laced waters
Through the white sleet
Followed by the flock with white wings flashing
And voices in the wind.
They walked away and never looked behind;
Never looked back at all.

Gravity

We live in black holes
Our instincts like lasers
God is redundant
Twixt time and quasars.

Brief and meaningless
Lives have we
Stardust to stardust
To be and not to be.

The Republic of Heaven
Shall not exist
Unless ye become
Like physicists.

But light and life
Are by gravity bent
So the answers are off
By X per cent

And counting quarks
On the head of a pin
Raises a slow
Angelic grin

And then my heart
With quantum ease
Goes dancing
With the galaxies.

The Metaphysical Poets
(For Mary Murphy, who teaches the teachers)

Outpouring words of light
Discomfort me,
Drowning in Spring and Autumn's vibrancy;
Immanent mystic might.

I cannot stillness seize
Nor bend my knee
In all the drama offered here to me,
With other's certainties.

I need to know that thrice
Denying souls
Have faults enough to circumvent the coals
And meet a smiling Christ.

The Comet

For a short while
We travelled out by night and reached
Grianan of Aileach,
The hilltop sun house of the Gods
And from within the massive storied walls
Shaded from all earth-light
We stood together
Star gazing from the ancient circle,
The clear black nights all riveted with stars.
And high above, there to the northwest
We found the comet, the unique glowing point
Tailed and then bearded by the solar wind.
Each night we tracked it on its path
And came to hold it, almost like a friend.
We did not know the meaning or the song
But we responded to it.
Through further midnight hours we watched with care
Its steady course across the field of stars
Past Ursa Major, Hercules and Lyra,
Then at a tangent, the bearing seemed to veer,
The glow to fade
And on the last night, slipping further away,
Leaving us,
We grasped for real that it would not return
For near two hundred years
And we would not be here
To welcome it.

I stood apart
And murmured a farewell,

Quiet and final as the stars
With an ineffable aching loss,
A lonely sadness, slow and still
And without solace
But for the passing of the years
And the way life drags you on.

The Point Of The Petunias
(For Ann)

In the soul of the wilderness there is a house
And on the kitchen worktop, a colour television
Solemnly telling of earth's magnetosphere
Pulsing around us like unseen lassoes
Taut with energy, whipping and crackling. Every
Two hundred thousand years or so, north becomes south,
Positive, negative, the polarity reverses suddenly.
'The proof of this is writ in the ancient rocks,'
Said the television in smooth God-like tones.
'When the whole thing flips over, the magnetic fields
Weaken and cosmic rays come flooding in.
It'll be pretty nasty,' said the voice of God.
'What's more, it's due to happen anytime now.
So watch it!' The moving finger wrote and then
The words slid neatly upwards, to solemn music.

To clear her cerebral cortex from the influence
Of these elegant and fearful imprecations,
She went out into the urban wilderness
And walked between the green pond and bamboos,
The leftover rocks, the raspberry canes, the sand heaps,
Tall-grown thickets, unpruned shrubs (these leaves,
She told herself, are all still free of tax)
And trees in terracotta pots, wind-tumbled.
She moved on her own path, trodden by herself,
Through her own wilderness, came with surprised delight
To freshly gifted flowers, glowing innocence
Under rippling bubble wrap, part of the great
Cosmic plan, waiting to be 'potted-on'.

She gazed in silence on the petunias,
Blue radiance in the swaying magnetic fields
And seriously debating back and forth.
She pursed her lips and slowly shook her head.

Auschwitz – Oswiecim – Birkenau

When I was four years old
Auschwitz was built.
Now, hesitant, I come,
Knowing the history
Of this fouled piece of earth
And see the single line of railway track
Stretch away through the brick archway of Birkenau,
The place of immediate death,
Of gas chambers and ovens
Or slower death from hunger and forced labour.

Arbeit macht frei.
Work sets you free
Written in iron.

And today a warm sun shines on those brick buildings;
On the avenues between;
On the square of death;
On the execution wall at Block Eleven;
On the few huge wooden barns still left
In the vast extermination field of Birkenau
Where one hundred thousand were held
At any given time.

Stand still here, in this enormous silence,
A sense of distance without echoes.
This place is empty;
Empty of people, prisoners, Jews and Poles;
Empty of terror, torture;
Empty of reason, of understanding

Or grasp of this unique evil
Which belongs
To our species only.
This vicious unkindness
Is of our kind.

And there is yet more:
Our brothers who committed this outrage
With such appalling method and precision,
And operating it in covert ways
Were Western,
White,
Intelligent,
Male,
Educated,
Disciplined,
Followers of the Christ,
And sane
As men all wish to be
Yet deaf and mute.

And the cries of despair;
O Yahweh, save us,
God have mercy on us.
Miserere nobis.
Let my people go.
Save our children,
Weeping,
Spare at least, the children;
And this in a babel of languages
From six million throats;
And there was no answer.
A terrible silence.

O God
If there is a God,
If prayer brings no response
We must make demands.
Speak to us.
We need an explanation
Of this horror;
This Holocaust.
What are you saying?
What is your meaning?
Is there a meaning?

Must we then believe this life, this world
Is a wasteland;
Godless,
Indifferent.
Rank
And meaningless,
As the numb, inhuman silence
Of Auschwitz-Birkenau?

Time Is Of The Essence

After his mother died, the physicist
With no belief in God, nor Paradise,
But expert in artificial consciousness,
Silenced his graduate class with his surmise.

'While consciousness is difficult to fix,
Illusion pervades everything. But when
Event horizons bend and stretch and mix
I'm sure to meet my mother once again.

'You see, the whole thing has to do with time
For time is not the same on Jupiter
And different in Andromeda or Orion,
It's complex space-time, relative and rare.

'Time swirls, comes round again. And this I know,
That she will hold my hand, as long ago.'

Postface
'Or singularly, perhaps it could be said,
That she has held my hand, long, long, long ahead.'

Och! Och! – The First Of January 2000

Along by Bay Park's river edge
The sky is massive.
The Foyle is a mile wide,

She came down to the river bank
Before the dawn
Alone,
On this first morning
Of the second millennium
To witness its first light of hope
And it was wet and cold and grey,
No sunrise edging through
The cracks in the clouds
The river flowing in indifferent anger
Echoed the sullen turbulence of the sky.

Under clouds of lead
She stood and waited there a while,
Expectant,
Half-expectant,
Then turned home disappointed
Out of sorts with all the world
And all the supernatural energies
Of its guardian spirits.

And no amount of talk about
The problems of a roseate dawn
Here in the harsh north
Of this stormy, spinning globe,
Nor yet the jet stream moving south

Dragging disturbances and polar air
Could mollify her indignant discontent,
Never mind, the whole thing flying round our star
At thirty kilometres per second.

For these things are not easy to accept
By a pilgrim searching for a sign of promise,
Seeking not explanations
But revelations.

‘Hmmph!’ she said,
‘Hmmph!’

Maggots

Wandering by Inch Lake
On one slow Autumn day
Looking around and taking
All the time there was,
Seeking a taste of childhood
I bit on a ripe red berry
From the fund on a hawthorn bush.
It tasted just the same
As fifty years before.
Delving and daring more
I sank a tooth into
A plump dark-purple sloe,
Bitter but darkly rich
With spicy overtones.
My tongue and mouth went dry
Same as when I was ten.
I found the antidote,
The annual bonus of fruit
Secure amongst the thorns
Hedging the briar bank
I picked a shining blackberry
(Remembering to check for maggots
Just as my granny taught me)
Tasted its watery sweetness
Juicing my mouth, restoring
Order to taste and tongue,
Confidence, liquidity.

I understand, on Wall Street,
They speak into their blackberries

To ease dry mouth and bitterness
While wild bears roam the market.
They take thought to themselves
To restore the established order,
Confidence, liquidity
Good taste and banker-speak
Just as they'd been taught
To avoid the fiscal wreck.
But somehow they forgot
To do the maggot check.

Inch Lake In November

The swans make down from northern climes
Over harsh seas without mistake
Under grey cloud they bank and climb
And sense their way by secret sign
Home to our sheltering Winter lakes.

Low-flying lakeside stubble-fields
Strong wings beat white against the sky
Full flocks of lapwing whirl and wheel
And greylag, mallard, wigeon, teal
Signal them down with fractious cries.

The yellow leaves fall thick and fast
Upon the grass and trodden way
Spring mornings stray into the past
And as the Summers may not last
The years go wandering away.

The Frequent Absolute

Here, with a glass in our weathered hands
Before our neurones soften,
Tell me, do you believe in God?
Of course I believe; quite often.

The Boy In The Morning
(In memory of Mickey McSorley, Manager
of Drumaweir House, 1947)

I laid two gleaming rabbit snares
Among the rocks and hammered in
The wooden pegs to hold the wires
Between the boulders and the whins

And in the morning light I went
To see what happened in the dawn
One snare was just as I had left,
Still fastened there, the other gone.

McSorley laughed, 'If I were you
I'd clear before he gets your number.
You tumbled the postman with your snare
And he's lookin' to choke the rabbit hunter.'

The Twilight Setting Pattern

(On receiving a star globe on my sixtieth birthday)

Men flying planes through evening sky
Seek out a star to travel by.
Men moving in our twilight state
Need seasoned aid to navigate.

Hence my delight, a pilgrim friend
Whose thoughts enable me transcend
Complexity and find a way
Through clouds of doubt and disarray

A poet from among green lanes
With deep Fermanagh in his veins
Whose cosmos flows beyond the fence
Of physics and intelligence.

He comes to me and sips my grain
And then, attempting to explain
With generosity presents
A star globe as a sacrament

And points me home as I research
The embers of my universe.

Hoar Frost

How rapidly the time has passed
The months like days, they turned so fast.
Are falling leaves like falling tears
When Autumn comes around at last?

How slowly do the childhood fears
Diminish, but not disappear
In spite of finding calmer days
Around the corners of the years.

And golden men and women may
Husband the fields and save the hay
Yet see beyond the harvest fire
The colours of another day.

When all the cows are in the byre
And grain is gathered, all entire
The present is become the past
With hard-won wisdom to inspire

Much greater things than lopping briars
When you retire, when you retire.

Bless Me, Father

A five-bar gate, slow rusting,
Climbed as a boy,
Lifted open for cattle,
Leaned on in later life.

Small fields of short grass,
Tough, weathered.
Walls of uncut rock.
The stream of air
Off the Atlantic
Sings through the stone.

Face into the wind
Scorning the shelter
Of whitethorn and fuchsia,
The figure at the gate
Stares towards Brooklyn,
Back turned to Glasgow,
Feet in Derrybeg,
The mind prospecting
Back and forth in time.

The search for meaning
Stumbles on small blessings,
Lasting grace,
In the fields and certainties
Of childhood.

The leaning figure,
Though changing generations

Looks back, sees forward,
Slow learning,
Discerning
The twin deceptions
Of success and failure.

Lean your elbows on the top bar,
Smoothed over the long years
By other arms,
Eyes watering in the wind,
Seeking and wondering.
Rest now awhile.

Inis Fail
(Lough Allen, February 2005)

Winter's end on this great lake.
Cloud rolling low, the waters grey
And massive flow by Drumleague Lock's
Huge limestone blocks, fitted and laid.
The New Year blossoms on jagged whins,
Yellow defiance amongst dark spikes
Sudden lights in the distant dim
Mountains and in the falling night
Three old sinners, of battered grace
Talk in the cabin, as years ago
Afloat in the dark with the stars ablaze
And Orion high over Drumshanbo
Argue the years in the light's declining
With a candle-full of whiskey,
Shining.

September

Once I was younger
Full of urgent promise.
I grew, as all do
Through the bruising years,
Learning as I went along
First to decipher, then discern
The story
From the storytelling.

Now I am weathered.
Changed.
I am an old thistle,
Fibrous, prickly, silver grey
And in the learning winds
My seedling thoughts soar high
Like thistledown
Seeking
The fertile ground
Where thoughts may bloom
Like sunflowers
And mine, maybe
Might have the luck
To make a meal
For goats.

Brief Candle

Our lives in three dimensions locked, confines
The light we can receive.
I would we might decipher whence it shines
Before we have to leave.

The Colours Of Another Day

For us who are weathered and chipped and worn
From hours both wise and unwise,
The thrush sings clear in the early morn
And it is almost sunrise.